JOY

OF BEING A WOMAN

THE

JOY

OF BEING A WOMAN

AMY HALL

STARK BOOKS
**Andrews McMeel
Publishing**
Kansas City

00 01 02 03 04 BIN 10 9 8 7 6 5 4 3 2 1

Library of Congress Cataloging-in-Publication Data
Hall, Amy.
  The joy of being a woman / Amy Hall.
      p. cm.
  ISBN 0-7407-1004-4 (pbk.)
    1. Women. 2. Femininity. 3. Women—Psychology. I. Title.

HQ1150 .H35 2000
305.4—dc21   00-55716

Book design by Holly Camerlinck

To a little girl who used to stay in from recess
and use the classroom typewriter to write stories

To Miss Stephanie, who had some faith

ACKNOWLEDGMENTS

A special thanks to these beloved contributors
who so kindly shared both their serious
and their sassy opinions on the joys of womanhood:

Cristina Bowerman	Scott Keepers
Ben Brenneman	Bil Kennedy
Lillian Butler	Karen Krueger
Karen Cohick	Jennifer Larson
Cristy Cooley	Carol Lefebure
Steve Davis	Martin LeRoy
Emily Flinn	Inge McCoy
Jennifer Flok	John McGuire
Evalyn Franzone	Julie McGuire
Leslie Faulkner Gage	Jennifer Mills
Lisa Garrison	Ken Milman
Kelly Gilbert	Marcy Milman
Susan Jennings	Gale Moore

Celine Oehrke

Terry Oehrke

Shannon Robb Park

Emöke Pulay

Melissa Raymond

Raphael Rios

Eric Slangerup

Sandy Smith

Roy Vargas

Felicia Waage

Brooke Ward

Brett Weiss

Julie Weiss

Mary Ann Wells

Scott Wells

INTRODUCTION

**One is not born a woman—
one becomes one.**

—*Simone de Beauvoir*

Being a woman is a wonderful, beautiful thing that offers an excellent opportunity for a joyous life. However, the world is full of chaos and frenzy, and there's not much chance that's going to change. The resulting downfall is we're so frantic with being good employees, spouses, daughters, mothers, and in-laws that sometimes we forget the simple, inalienable joys of life—the joys of being a woman! This book is to remind gals everywhere of how delicious the experience of womanhood is and of the little quirks that make the feminine adventure so unique. Now grab some chocolate, put your feet up, and read on!

THE

JOY

OF BEING A WOMAN

You can particularly savor

the delicious release and

relaxation that comes from getting

a great manicure. I personally feel like

a queen for the rest of the day

on which I treat myself to one.

Saying "I told you so" to a good friend
when she finally breaks down and has a kid
just like you knew she would.

&

You can be physically affectionate with your
girlfriends, hugging them all day long
without a bit of embarrassment.

&

There are wonderful fathers in the world
for certain, but no one can nurture
quite like a woman.

You appreciate the stature of being a woman in modern America—we've simply never had the power we have now, and it's growing. I'm ever appreciative of this fact and feel that younger women should not take for granted all the laws and programs now available that protect our interests and needs. We didn't always have such great perks as maternity leave or funding for women's sports.

THE
JOY
OF BEING A WOMAN

You know in your heart you never used anyone for sex. (Well, okay, we're allowed that one time!)

You feel good about showing emotions. You inherently know it's important.

Less body hair. Please don't dare force me to elaborate!

You can do the splits!
(And if your name is Emöke,
you do them at wedding receptions.)

❧

The ecstasy of the female orgasm
has yet to be explained or duplicated in
a lab and remains a beautiful thing of
mystery. (Can you say, "Oh yeah, baby!")

A woman may develop
wrinkles and cellulite,
lose her waistline, her bustline,
her ability to bear a child,
even her sense of humor,
but none of that implies a loss
of sexuality, her femininity.

—*Barbara Gordon, TV producer and writer*

Enjoying your husband or boyfriend's
slight discomfort as another man
completely checks you out and is perhaps
even brash enough to flirt with you a bit.

❧

Wearing skintight pants.
There's nothing like throwing a pair on
to distress your mother-in-law
during Sunday brunch at the
Opryland Hotel.

Spending exorbitant amounts of money on bath products and luxurious lotions. I simply can't get out of a Bath & Body Works store without dipping into my retirement savings in the process. Because of this phenomenon, I'm beginning to suspect that all such products are laced with some type of addictive additive that seeps into women's skin and leaves them begging for just one more little bottle of apple-scented shower gel.

In a modern American bar,
you can offer to buy a guy a drink.

❧

You're completely eligible to fully
participate in "girl talk" discussions.
There's nothing like being privy
to the camaraderie of women. And at no
other forum could the topics of
cookie baking, in-laws, and oral sex
all be addressed within a ten-minute
time span.

You have that one great skirt

that puts you on top of the world—

forget about stuffy power suits!

My friend Melissa has a little black number

that simply leaves men on their knees.

She wears it in the spirit of true vixenhood,

and I always say more power to her.

Your spending habits and criteria for
buying consumer products are currently
becoming the basis for all product
development and tailoring—your
comfort and approval are paramount
in the eyes of industry.

❧

Finding a pair of control-top panty hose
in the recesses of your underwear drawer
when you're bloated with your period

Having a sister you love and
appreciating her role as a female comrade
in your life

Sending kids to camp for the entire
summer and relishing the impact
it could have on your sex life

Childbirth is more admirable than conquest, more amazing than self-defense, and as courageous as either one.

—*Gloria Steinem, American feminist, editor, and writer*

We have extraordinary bodies; a woman is simply nature's work of art. The classic curves of our breasts and hips are breathtaking and remain sensual throughout our lives.

❦

Shopping on the Internet at 2:00 A.M. when you can't sleep. (jjill.com and eddiebauer.com, why doest thou tempt me and my credit card so?)

Wearing flowers in your hair just because

❧

Discovering a panty hose brand that actually
lasts for more than two wears and buying
some in every available color

Taking your kids to the zoo

and seeing their delight as they explore

and exclaim, and appreciating that they

reawaken your own wonder at

the incredible world in which we live

Knowing if you want to join the military,
you can. You have the power of choice.

☙

Your charms and feminine wiles
ensure that no request you make of the
opposite sex will ever be denied.
(I once got my taxes done for free
at H & R Block, enough said.)

☙

Multiple orgasms, hear me roar.

Overpacking for every vacation
or weekend jaunt you will ever take
in your entire life and driving
our significant other mad in the process

❧

If you feel self-conscious about
being short, you can wear high heels
and no one thinks a thing of it.

I've always believed

that one woman's success

can only help another

woman's success.

—*Gloria Vanderbilt, fashion designer*

We can wear tons of pretty, elegant jewelry and accessories. I'm all for sapphires and really good scarves.

Freely admitting you like the hottest new love song

You can bear children if you so wish.
A man can't quite go it alone.

A fifty-dollar facial never looked so good
pasted upon your face

Washing your hands of fad diets once
and for all and simply focusing on leading
a healthy lifestyle

If we have a zit,
we know how to conceal it.

We have a lot of freedom
when it comes to expressing and
exploring our creativity. We can learn
a craft, take a painting class, redecorate
our homes, start ballroom dancing,
or do whatever else it takes to keep our
imaginative juices flowing.

You have breasts, and breasts are just
plain cool. I confess I am ever fascinated
with my bosom. Don't get the wrong idea,
Victoria's Secret will never hire me
for a commercial—I just simply love
my breasts because they're all mine!

⚜

Maternity leave

⚜

Pampering our bodies is not seen as unusual.
Foofy maybe, unusual no.

If you want anything said,

ask a man.

If you want anything done,

ask a woman.

—*Margaret Thatcher, first woman prime minister*
of England

Realizing how much larger and more
mature your child suddenly appears
on her birthday and wondering where
in the world the past year has gone

❧

Once a month, we can eat our way
across the Americas and to China and back
and declare our hormones made us do it.
(For whatever reason, I must always
have chicken fried rice and something
with walnuts at this particular time.)

Looking so cute in the chic sunglasses
you spent weeks searching for. And if
you're my friend Brooke, you spent at least
two months looking around.

✂

The pride you feel after finishing
your first home improvement project
or car repair all on your own. (I recently
felt gobs more talented than Bob Vila
after I neatly caulked a foot-long seam
in my kitchen.)

Never feeling self-conscious
while reading *People* in public

✇

Sitting down with a wonderful book
by a great female author such as
Jane Austen, Agatha Christie, or
Flannery O'Connor

✇

Celebrating friends' birthdays
by remembering to give them a call,
a card, or a gift

THE

JOY

OF BEING A WOMAN

We get through airport security easier than men. (A male friend of mine was very emphatic and bitter about this, and I had to agree it's a fact. My spouse has been stopped by airport security a million times. I've only been stopped once, and I would swear it was because the guard felt like flirting a wee bit.)

Nonchalantly buying self-help books
at the bookstore. I can walk up to the
cash register with *Chicken Soup for the Soul,*
tantric sex manuals, and *You Can Heal
Your Life* and not think twice about
the clerk flipping through them.

❧

Acting scared during a movie
so you can latch on to your date
(Hey, we all need an entry point.)

If one could be friendly

with a woman, what a pleasure—

the relationship so secret

and private compared with

relations of men.

—*Virginia Woolf, English novelist*

Sending loving cards to our friends
and relatives (and in the process wishing
we could have invested in Hallmark
years ago!)

❧

Having a stash of "fat clothes"
to help us out when we've been a bit too
active with our forks and spoons

❧

Patting yourself on the back
for being thoughtful

Being held and kissed by a man
(Hey, a little romp never hurt anyone
either, right?)

You can be called Mom.

We have total emotional freedom.
We can cry when we want.
We can laugh when we want. We can
be catty hussies when we want.

Rubbing your silky smooth legs
after you just shaved them in a bath

Looking nymphlike in those
great summer sundresses

Dabbing on a touch of lip gloss
or Chap Stick

Understanding the importance

of owning an ungodly multitude

of black pants and skirts

(May the monochrome police never

search my closet.)

Women are always being tested . . .
but ultimately, each of us
has to define who we are
individually and then do the
very best job we can.

—*Hillary Rodham Clinton, attorney
and former First Lady*

THE
JOY
OF BEING A WOMAN

Having sexy lingerie tucked away
for those special occasions when you
want to surprise your lover

❧

Saving up enough money to finally
take the vacation of your dreams,
be it rappelling down cliffs in South
America or sucking down margaritas on
a cruise ship. (I'm hankering to see
Costa Rica and Australia.)

Day care, take me away.
(Sometimes, even the Brady Bunch
needed some space from one another.)

We don't believe that whoever dies
with the most complex remote control wins.

Finding that special peace that comes

when tending our gardens and indoor plants.

There's nothing that relaxes me more

than when I make time to go

baby my honeysuckle vines and

Climbing Blush rosebush.

Experimenting with eye shadow
and not ending up bearing a striking
resemblance to a raccoon

Wearing a god-awful bridesmaid dress
because you love your friend so much
you forgive her sudden lack of taste

Getting even with all your girlfriends
by selecting the tackiest bridesmaid dresses
available when *you* get married

❧

No matter how bad life may seem at
any given time, knowing you could
at least drum up a blind date arrangement
sure to leave you laughing for
the next two months

Spending tons of time

selecting candles to purchase—

there's just a science to it. I simply

have to smell every one at the display rack

or I know the world as we know it

could possibly come to an end.

She didn't know it couldn't be done

so she went ahead and did it.

—*Mary's Almanac*

Reading all the enlightening articles in *Playgirl* (I love occasionally purchasing one of these babies for a shy friend. Why? [A] The teenage guy cashier always blushes. [B] My shy friend acts all disgusted that I have purchased such trash for her and then proceeds to cover the magazine with a fine-tooth comb for the next two hours straight.)

THE

JOY

OF BEING A WOMAN

Elevating shopping to an Olympic sport

✿

Feeling that butterfly sensation when
a baby starts to move around inside you

✿

Slipping into your faithful bathrobe
after stepping out of a bath, no matter
how tattered the world may consider it

✿

Freely ordering fruity drinks like
amaretto sours or strawberry daiquiris
at bars

✿

Participating in some innocent flirtation
during red lights from the seat of
your snazzy new car (I recently got
an electric blue convertible and am
so happy to have my roadside
sex appeal back!)

Getting all pumped up and sweaty
while playing some intense
women's sports

❧

Cheaper car insurance
(However, I've heard rumors this perk
is really just society's way of helping
offset the expense of tampons,
panty hose, and makeup.)

Mother Nature granted us a
longer life expectancy since we're much
less destructive to the earth.

✼

Our sex reaches physical and
emotional maturity quicker than
our male counterpart.

A grown woman

did not need safety

or its dreams.

She was the safety

she longed for.

—*Toni Morrison, writer and novelist*

Taking zany photographs of our friends
and the events of our lives

❧

Maintaining a sense of spirituality
despite all the difficulty and stress
modern life throws our way. Sometimes
this is harder than usual, but I believe
women are uniquely talented at keeping
this area of their lives very much
in check.

If you're feeling bored with life,
you could just wear some pasties
on your nipples and see if anything
interesting happens.

We can be tomboys. We can toss on
our baseball caps and jeans and
fix the house or play first base with
the best of them.

Experiencing the special tie
between mothers and daughters

❧

Chocolate. Women fully appreciate the
sensual and rich flavor of this blessed
and sacred food product. We're true
aficionados who can fluently lecture
about the advantages of creamy versus
dark, Swiss versus English, et cetera.

(Long live the Hershey's Kiss!)

THE
JOY
OF BEING A WOMAN

Ordering something from a catalog and feeling giddy at the sight of any UPS truck you see for the next week (and then finally having that *studly* deliveryman tenderly place an L. L. Bean or J. Crew package in your anxious little paws)

Sequins. When the occasion arises,
we love to slap 'em on.

❧

Fuzzy house slippers

❧

Surviving being a wedding planner
for your girlfriends

The roosters may crow,

but the hens deliver the goods.

—*Ann Richards, politician*

Enraging controlling parents and
future in-laws by eloping to Vegas

❧

Girls drop out of school less than
their male counterparts and are now
the reigning majority of those seeking
advanced degrees at colleges and
universities across the nation.

Helping heal our friends and families
when they're ill

We know love is more valuable than
any currency or territory line.

Admitting that on some days you like food
better than sex (especially when anything
Italian is on the menu! [insert purr here])

❧

Actually knowing how to insert
a new roll of toilet paper on the holder
in the bathroom

The unspoken connection you have
with your children, of which they aren't
even aware. You're totally plugged into
their joys and pains in a surreal manner
you can barely explain to others.

Letting it all go through a good cry,
and I mean the kind where the
floodgates are *wide* open

Blowing bubbles along with your youngsters

❧

Understanding the chemistry behind
the fact that on some days
a garden salad, diet soda, and piece
of Chocolate Kamikaze Suicide Death Cake
make a balanced lunch

Work by a male writer is often

spoken of by critics admiring it as

having "balls"; ever hear anyone

speak admiringly of work by a

woman as having "tits"?

—*Margaret Atwood, Canadian poet and novelist*

Finally reaching some common ground
with your mother-in-law

❧

Being an aunt. It's all the idyllic warm
fuzzies of parenthood with none of the
birds and bees seminars, allowance
negotiations, or tantrum mediations.

❧

The day your child proudly hands you
her first report card

Trying on your bathing suit in
early spring to discover you haven't put on
that much winter weight

✣

We know the dark sides and drives
of all our fellow women. This is info
which men would pay millions
of dollars for but which, of course,
we'll never betray.

In the free world, we can now vote.
We can also strive to help our sisters
who cannot assert this glorious privilege.

❧

Believing that our manicurist treats us
better than any blind date we've ever
been subjected to

❧

We can fake it. (Insert evil, maniacal
laugh that chills men's spines here.)

Making time to pursue childhood dreams
that fell by the wayside. I recently
started taking piano lessons again,
and I'm so loving it.

❧

Passing on a family treasure
to your daughter, be it linens and china
or simply your own tattered teddy bear
from childhood

Everything you see,

I owe to spaghetti.

—*Sophia Loren, actress*

THE
JOY
OF BEING A WOMAN

Debutante balls—if you don't have one,
you can at least make fun of them
till the sun comes up.

Being a daddy's girl. And I'll admit
I've been the world's worst. It's very hard
for my father to do any wrong
in my eyes, and I think he knows
I could still talk him into anything
if I batted my eyelashes a bit!

Spending a leisurely day shopping

to get away from it all and get yourself

a few treats. I'm not one to exalt

mindless activity, but sometimes I think

it's totally healthy and necessary

to stroll around a mall completely

brain-dead in order to escape the

hubbub some particular weeks bring.

THE

JOY

OF BEING A WOMAN

Anthropologists assert the female body is sturdier and built to withstand more than the male body.

Vamping repair guys in order to get a cheaper bill (As my friend Lillian puts it, "Do you have any 'damsel in distress' specials today?" [insert wink here])

You have the best excuse to quit
your job and stay home—children.

Having the myriad of birth control options
modern science provides

An honest friend saying,
"Gosh, your kids are so cool."

Watching a WNBA game

with your superathletic daughter

No one stares when you go to the bathroom

with a friend.

She knew what
all smart women knew:
Laughter made you live better
and longer.

—*Gail Parent, scenarist*

THE

JOY

OF BEING A WOMAN

Inhaling your kids' leftovers after dinner
and attributing it to the fact that you
"just couldn't let it all go to waste"

⁂

Getting some popcorn and kicking back
to watch a great "chick flick" like
Boys on the Side or *Beaches*

Subjecting your significant other
to watching a "chick flick" with you

❦

Flirting with your waiter (C'mon, admit it.
We all know we get better service when
we work our stuff.)

❦

Relying on our friends to tell us
when there's spinach or lipstick
on our teeth

Going to school reunions and
happily discovering that the once rude
and beautiful no longer have any
power over you

The ability to be sexy, smart,
funny, sensitive, and strong
all at the same time

Throwing baby showers.

What better way to distract

your pregnant loved one from her

immobility than by having her sit down

for a long time to open tons of gifts

for that creature whose sonograms

are plastered all over the fridge?

Donning a slinky velvet dress
for a holiday party

❧

Receiving thoughtful gifts
and homemade goodies from your family
on Mother's Day

Just go out there

and do what you've got to do.

—*Martina Navratilova, tennis legend*

THE

JOY

OF BEING A WOMAN

Seductively eating an ice cream cone

❧

Watching your mom and aunts go back to
do things they couldn't do at your age

❧

Seeing women win good purses on the
LPGA tour

Miracle bras (a.k.a. Add water,
instant risk-free boob job)

✘

Tucking tags into the backs
of our friends' blouses and having them
be so grateful

✘

Watching *When Harry Met Sally.*
This is my all-time favorite movie
to watch with a friend.

We live in an era where our sisters

who are physically or mentally abused

by their husbands can divorce and suffer

no entailing social stigma as they move on

to brighter places.

Releasing some of the stress of the
workday by indulging in just a teeny bit
of road rage on the drive home

❧

Cracking Lorena Bobbitt jokes
in front of men

Calling your best friend

to tell her you finally lost your virginity

(and then eventually getting this

same call from her—within two weeks

if she's the competitive type)

I thank God for my handicaps, for through them, I have found myself, my work, and my God.

—*Helen Keller, American essayist and lecturer*

Wearing seamless underwear.
There's nothing finer for showing off
your rear.

❧

Being Joan of Arc to the lady you meet
in the bathroom who's in need
of a tampon

❧

Becoming a crazy cat lady and spending
all your social security money on Cat Chow
(I am so well on my way to this!)

❧

Shopping at Victoria's Secret.

You always feel so seductive and decadent

when you walk out the door

with something. (ALERT! ALERT!

Overpowering advertising campaign and

fancy catalogs have brainwashed author.

ALERT! ALERT!)

THE

JOY

OF BEING A WOMAN

Speaking bluntly about your
problematic sex life with girlfriends
without being embarrassed in any way

⚘

Discovering a clearance sale
in your favorite store

⚘

Receiving beautiful family heirlooms
to cherish and call your own

Hiding a trashy romance novel
under the bed that only you know you
are reading (Now, if only we can find
a man with half as much stamina
as those Casanovas who romp our
distressed fictional heroines.)

Not suffering the inconvenience of
having to constantly protect your ovaries
(versus the ongoing and zealous effort
required of any man wanting to keep
his testicles safe and intact)

❧

Participating in feminist activism
to keep women's issues at the forefront
of politics

To be somebody,

a woman does not

have to be more like a man

but has to be

more like a woman.

—*Sally Shaywitz, pediatrician and writer*

Getting a great pedicure at your favorite salon. I'm certain there are statistics somewhere proving that women truly relax and feel all sensual after having one of these performed. I positively melt into my seat and let everything go when a pedicurist works on my feet.

That special period when your
children *actually* think you're an
excellent singer as you lullaby them
while they're drifting off to sleep

❧

Seeing female coaches lead teams
to sweet victory and sportsmanlike losses
and actually be paid for it.
Go Pat Summitt and Jody Conradt!

Getting a cell phone so you can blab
even more with your girlfriends

✣

Never being forced to make conversation
with the person next to you in a public
bathroom while you're urinating

✣

Knowing the importance of having
stashes of Advil

Putting up with the woman beside you
in the checkout line who is annoyed
by your crying children and knowing that
somewhere, someday she'll regret it

The glamour and splendor of red
nail polish on your toes.
(I like 'em as fire engine red
as I can get 'em.)

Someone little coming up to you
and saying, "You're the best mommy
in the whole world."

❧

Browsing through the sex toys store
and finding something interesting

I don't have the time

every day to put on makeup.

I need that time to clean my rifle.

—*Henriette Mantel, actress*

We can get stuffed animals as gifts
all our lives.

❧

Witnessing the era of men being
expected to help with housework

❧

Having throwaway Pampers or Huggies
in your baby's room. You just can't knock
anything that removes tons of poop
from your life so conveniently.

Celebrating the range of professional

positions now open to women

and picking out the one that's just right

for you, or taking the plunge to

become self-employed (I will warn you

that the latter is scary at first,

but sometimes you simply have to

take chances with your life.)

Diamonds

＊

Big diamonds

＊

Distastefully large diamonds

Putting away enough money in your piggy bank to finally be able to fly to the wonderful friend who somehow ended up hundreds of miles away (Fortunately for me, Chicago is a relatively close city.)

THE

JOY

OF BEING A WOMAN

Flipping through the never-shrinking
stack of artwork your child has
created for you

❧

Keeping up the charade that we're
incapable of heavy labor and letting
men perform it instead. Coincidentally,
life insurance companies are just amazed
at our longer life expectancies—go figure!

I have a brain and a uterus,

and I use both.

—*Patricia Schroeder, president of the*
Association of American Publishers
and former congresswoman

Showing your youngsters a picture of yourself when you were a little girl and watching the surprise and incomprehension unfold. It's really hard for them to believe that, three trillion years ago, you too were once young and wild.

The rush of egomania we felt
that first time we wore a tampon.
We'd never been cooler in our minds' eyes.

Those glorious afternoons when your
husband says, "Honey, I'll watch the kids,
you go relax for a little while and
do something fun."

The sensual and decadent sensation
of dabbing perfume on your wrists
and neck. (I believe in having a perky
fruity scent for the daytime, and something
really musky for presex seductions.)

❧

The amazement we have with our bodies
as we cycle to the rhythms of the moon
and oceans

Taking a cheating husband
for all he's worth after watching
The First Wives Club, then going on
with your life

Catching a game of women's soccer

THE

JOY

OF BEING A WOMAN

Having a linen chest full of our special treasures. On rainy days, it's fun to peruse our past by flipping through long-forgotten letters, childhood toys, wedding photographs, diplomas, and other special tokens from our lives.

Knowing you're always in control of your man and just letting him think he's making all the decisions (I found it amusing that nearly all the people I polled about the joys of womanhood mentioned this.)

Munching on some

Godiva chocolate-covered

strawberries

THE

JOY

OF BEING A WOMAN

Once women pass fifty, if they can avoid the temptations of the eternal youth purveyors, the sellers of unnatural thinness and cosmetic surgery, they may be able to tap into the feisty girls they once were.

—*Carolyn Heilbrun, writer and educator*

Proudly knowing our sex designed
comfort food. Forget the elaborate
creations of the world's great male chefs.
On a bad day, all anyone truly wants is
a crisp grilled cheese, a humongous
crockpot full of soup, or a fat stack
of pancakes.

❧

Collecting your thoughts in a journal.
Because I'm a writer, this has become
an important activity to me by default, but
I think it's something everyone should
explore in order to analyze her feelings
and goals.

THE

JOY

OF BEING A WOMAN

A man's basis for proposing marriage to you
is no longer based on your hip width
and cooking skills.

❧

Bridal showers. Attending them and
organizing them is an important rite of
passage for every woman, no matter how
goofy the theme or the games played.
But the best part is someone special goes
home with a great stash of domestic
products and trashy lingerie feeling all loved.

❧

Ribbed condoms—you gotta love 'em.

If you wake up looking ghastly,
you can disguise yourself in makeup.

✖

Brad Pitt

✖

Slipping on a favorite pair of
blue jeans after slipping out of yet
another pair of panty hose that
proved threatening to your circulation

Keeping up your sense of humor
during menopause with lots of
hot-flash jokes

❧

Making our female ancestors proud
by graduating from high school, college,
law school, and medical school
in record numbers—places most of them
couldn't even dream of attending

Women are the glue

that holds our day-to-day

world together.

—Anna Quindlen, journalist and

Pulitzer Prize winner

Playing bunko with the girls and
actually winning the pot

※

We don't have to memorize and
continuously quote lines from the
Die Hard trilogy, *Weird Science*, *Caddyshack*,
Terminator, *Ace Ventura*, or *Austin Powers*
in order to fit in with our peers.

※

Slipping on the delicate bracelet that
hangs on your wrist so elegantly

Women who follow people around
are groupies; men who follow people
around are stalkers.

❧

Playing matchmaker for desperate
single friends

❧

Playing matchmaker for desperate
single friends, actually watching it succeed,
then thinking how surprised you are

You get to wear sexy dresses.
Long ones, short ones, black ones,
red ones—you name it!

❧

Having a sense of awe while watching
your pregnant belly expand. Incidentally,
this is a time when you become really
interested in how you look from the side
in mirrors. (I have to totally confess
while we're on this topic that I love
seeing my friends and acquaintances
while they're pregnant. I just can never
get over how adorable they all look.)

Slipping on a feather boa,
just to make things interesting

❧

Virgin sacrifices are a thing of the past.

Women and elephants

never forget.

—*Dorothy Parker, writer and humorist*

Beating other women to the best
bargains during after-Christmas sales
at Target

※

Dressing all smutty for Halloween
(I'll never forget the year I was a
devil temptress.)

※

Living in blissful ignorance concerning
the importance of extensive
home theater systems

Avoiding subjection to the terrible
"cough test" during your annual physical

❧

Bachelorette parties (Can you say
"Pass me the one-dollar bills
for the stripper and that gin bottle
you got over there?")

Having a weekly lunch date with one of your best girlfriends. If I'd only been able to write down the top ten joys of being a woman instead of listing five hundred, this is one wonderful thing that would definitely have made the cut. There is nothing so delicious as sitting down with a buddy and talking each other's ears off in an hourlong heart-to-heart. (Cheers to you, Leslie!)

Meeting your girlfriend's baby
for the first time and seeing how
the new mother is so proud
(even though the newborn does look
a *little* alienlike)

The glass ceiling dissolving
when you finally got the promotion
you deserved over the man who didn't

Making peace with our mothers

Knowing most world religions

started out as goddess worship

(What the hell happened?)

I think a single woman's

biggest problem is coping

with the people who are trying to

marry her off!

—*Helen Gurley Brown, publisher*

Being the fun and zany grandma
little kids seek. It's not just about
baking cookies; it's about the special,
loving friendship that only you can foster
with your children's children.

❧

Condemning the inaccuracy of every
bathroom scale in existence
(especially in January, after all the
holiday parties have wrapped up)

Strategically placing boxes of
Kleenex anywhere you could ever
conceivably need them

Limp is a word that certainly fills
us with disappointment,
but not heart-stopping fear.

Seeing your son pick out
a decent woman to marry

Watching your adult daughter achieve
a goal set years before

❧

The very existence of tampons

❧

Knowing that if all else fails,
there would be at least three hundred
ultra-lonely men in line to marry you
if you moved to the more remote
areas of Alaska

Your first paycheck
(Elizabeth Cady Stanton would be
so proud)

❧

Returning terrible wedding gifts
and then having a huge credit
with the Pottery Barn or JCPenney
that you *have* to spend

You can take no credit

for beauty at sixteen.

But if you are beautiful at sixty,

it will be your soul's

own doing.

—*Marie Stopes, English women's activist*

and author

Wearing a strand of pearls

❧

Meeting the man of your dreams
and seeing no wedding band

❧

Watching *Oprah* and doing everything
Oprah says to do and reading everything
she says to read and buying everything
she says to buy. Why? Because Oprah
is lord of all that is sensible and good.

Scraping your girlfriend off the floor
at a bar and taking her home
because you know she'd do it for you

Really knowing why women go
to the bathroom together

Reading trashy fashion magazines
to make you brain-dead after a
way too stressful day

Being able to understand the phrase
"period panties" in a conversation

Spending the day at a spa
and feeling decadent

Leopard print accessories (as long as you
don't go crazy with them)

Not being expected to change a flat tire.
Long live overly tight lug nuts!

How wrong is it for a woman

to expect the man to build

the world she wants, rather than

set out to create it herself.

—*Anaïs Nin, French novelist and diarist*

The ultimate high you experience
after giving birth, no matter how long
or painful your labor may have been.
Suddenly before you is this tiny creature
who has been depending on you
for everything, and who will
completely change your life.

❧

Having superior eyesight that allows us
to detect the difference between
cream, ivory, and off-white.

THE
JOY
OF BEING A WOMAN

Bringing out the box of hot chocolate
the first morning the cold weather hits

❧

Knowing which glass is yours by
the lipstick mark (Of course, we have
to admit that at larger dinner parties,
this can become a fairly gross process
of elimination.)

Having a choice whether to have

a career, or have kids and stay home,

or have kids and a career, or have kids

and a career from home, or stay home

and do nothing, or get sterilized

and trek the Himalayas, or . . .

(insert endless possibilities here)

Proudly seeing your children finally go off
into the world, knowing you've given them
everything you possibly could

❧

Getting sucked into watching QVC
or Home Shopping Network broadcasts
in the wee hours

Asking a man to dance, because it
really surprises the heck out of them

❧

Automated tongues
(If you have to ask, don't.)

Those special moments of connection you have with good girlfriends.

One very cold Chicago night, I stood alongside my beloved Dora on the top floor of the Hancock Observatory looking across the never-ending lights of the city and the pitch black darkness of Lake Michigan.

We weren't really talking, we were just standing there together, and I was overcome by the amazing sense of how deeply I cared for her as my best friend and of how far we had each ventured in life. Taking in the amazing scene before us was simply a beautiful moment for me. I later realized that I've had similar moments with other special friends over the years, and I think all women should take a minute to think about the instances when time stopped as they were in the presence of a treasured comrade and the beauty of the world.

When men reach their sixties

and retire, they go to pieces.

Women just go right on cooking.

—*Gail Sheehy, writer and social critic*

Relishing the extra personal space
people give you the week you're PMS-ing

You never have to pretend
that contacts are bothering you
or there is dirt in your eyes.
You can just cry.

Having an endless "need" for new shoes and clothes. You simply never have enough, which is a great reason to be continually shopping around for fresh articles of attire.

Girls' Night Out (a.k.a. Let's party like we did before we had minivans and mortgages.)

Sneaking a peek at some greased-up Chippendale's studs

The luxury of being able to openly confess how much you're interested in theater, art, and music

❧

You have the option not to change your last name when you get married nowadays. If nothing else, it's good for offending your mother-in-law right from the start.

❧

Kegel exercises (one-two-three, one-two-three)

Spending the afternoon with a girlfriend
so you can help dye each other's hair

❧

Taking lots of bubble baths (I say at least
three a week never hurt anybody.)

A woman who is willing

to be herself and pursue

her own potential runs

not so much the risk of loneliness

as the challenge of exposure

to more interesting men—

and people in general.

—*Lorraine Hansberry, playwright*

You can mess with a man's testosterone
count just by dressing like a hussy.

❧

"But I might break my nails"
is a great excuse to get out of all kinds
of petty tasks.

The relief of consulting a psychologist
to help you work through the frustrations
of daily life

❧

Demonstrating to your husband
that you can in fact connect a
TV and a VCR

Making a difference in your community
by volunteering with your favorite charity
group or at your child's school

Seeing your kids get off the school bus
and start sprinting toward the front door

Showing off your engagement ring
(admit it!)

Not buying into the hype that you lose your attractiveness and sense of sexuality as you pass through birthdays; instead opting to celebrate the fact that every year you become more and more of a vital and sensual woman (If I hear one more completely beautiful and talented woman complain about hitting thirty or forty, I'm going to smack her! I simply can't stand some women treating themselves so poorly in this regard!)

THE

JOY

OF BEING A WOMAN

Just when you thought it couldn't get any more fun, you find out you're having another child.

You'll never be bored. If all else fails, you can shop for eight hours.

Never grow a wishbone,

daughter, where a backbone

ought to be.

—*Clementine Paddleford, journalist and editor*

Finding your girlhood diary,

full of its innocent hopes and

touching naïveté, and rejoicing

in the little girl you once were

Enhancing the size of your breasts
just by selecting a different bra for the day

❧

We have a good excuse to play hooky
from work once a month.

❧

You can start out with nothing,
get married then divorced, and end up
with half of everything.

The private nature of a woman being
sexually aroused. Anyone just looking
would never be able to tell for certain;
thus, our exquisite aura of mystery
is well preserved.

❧

Women and children are always
evacuated first in the event
of an emergency.

Knowing why it's good to have
at least twelve different pairs
of black shoes

Munching on chocolate chip cookies
you pulled from the oven before
anyone could pounce on them
(It's just too darn tempting.)

The power of knowing one tiny

birth control pill renders

twenty trillion sperm ineffective

(BWWWAAAHAHAHHAHAH

[that was an evil laugh in case

you couldn't tell])

Corsets are no longer in style.

I'm not afraid of storms,

for I'm learning how to

sail my ship.

—Louisa May Alcott, writer

That delicious sneaky feeling
that comes from not wearing a bra
(I admit that I go *au naturel* whenever
I think I can get away with it.
My petty little life needs whatever jolt
I can give it!)

Playing around in the house and yard
one day, not bothering to shower,
fix your hair, or do a darn thing
to yourself

Having everything a drag queen wants

You can compete in the Olympics
in synchronized swimming.

Making your husband check out
all the scary sounds at night while you
stay curled up under the blankets.

❦

Dishwashers now being standard issue
in all homes

❦

Renting *Thelma & Louise*
(It's just a woman thing.)

Seeing that teenage pregnancy
is on the decline

✣

Bitching and crying about everything
with your best friend until 2:00 A.M.
and her assuring you that it's all
going to be okay

Striving to be a good role model
to younger women. I'm trying my best
at this for my niece. I'm of course
nowhere near perfect, but I think
everybody has to help make up for the
moral slack left by the trashy pop-culture
figures kids worship on the TV.

How many cares one loses

when one decides not to be

something, but to be someone.

—*Coco Chanel, French couturier*

Sweet memories of Girl Scoutdom

❧

Those great Girl Scout cookies
we can still pig out on

❧

Screaming along to Aretha Franklin's
"Respect" while cruising through
rush-hour traffic (It's also fun to
ignore the stares from fellow drivers
who think you're an interstate
concert freak.)

THE
JOY
OF BEING A WOMAN

You have a refreshing variety
of options when it comes to
dressing yourself. You actually get
to express some creativity
and individuality.

✣

Watching *The Rosie O'Donnell Show*

✣

You're a sexy cigar smoker.

Young girls' rising math and science scores

Witnessing the confidence and
esteem generated by women and girls
involved in sports together

THE
JOY
OF BEING A WOMAN

Knowing an epidural is available at
your request (I've never seen
a pregnant woman wear a
"Don't Do Drugs" T-shirt!)

✿

Valentine's Day—the one day of the year
when our significant others
might think about possibly attempting
to be romantic and thoughtful.
If nothing else, there's at least a
better-than-average chance we'll get
some better-than-average sex.

They say that inside

every fat woman

is a skinny woman

waiting to get out.

Well, all I can say is,

I ate that bitch.

—*Thea Vidale, comedienne*

Finding a thoughtful gift for a friend
or lover while shopping (It sounds silly,
but my husband gets giddy if I just
bring him home some sour candy.)

Having at least eight potpourri
containers scattered throughout the house.
Setting up some sweet smells is a great way
to mask the fact you haven't really
cleaned your house in five months.

Seeing women musicians now succeeding
in an industry that has traditionally
placed their talents on the back burner

❦

You never see any female
Elvis impersonators. Period.

❦

Arranged marriages are very out of style.

Maid service isn't just
for rich women anymore.

※

Having lots of foofy pillows scattered
across the bed and letting your husband
try to figure out the importance of this
on his own (It cracks me up how no man
I know ever gets this.)

※

Slipping into those ratty flannel jammies
you can't bear to trash

Having a savvy female boss to mentor
and groom you (Thank you, S.J. and S.B.—
my own two gurus.)

Free drinks, free dinners, free movies—
you get the point. But if you want to pay,
that's okay, too.

I was elected by the women

of Ireland, who instead of

rocking the cradle,

rocked the system.

—*Mary Robinson, first woman president*

of Ireland

Celebrating when you finally

find THE perfect man (or woman).

At last, a new age begins

where you can fart openly,

eliminate makeup, spoon every night,

and simply relax.

Really appreciating butterflies

Shopping for your wedding dress. It's a fun thing to do and the expression on your face when you first look into a mirror all dressed in white is priceless.

Finding the ideal purse

It's not difficult to get a taxi.
Drivers will pass three men waving money
if they see you at the end of the block
with your leg outstretched.

Exalting in the fact Freud
(that friggin' pervert) admitted he
never quite figured us out

THE

JOY

OF BEING A WOMAN

Knowing a good man is hard to find,
but an impeccable hairdresser
damn near impossible

✣

Since men die so much earlier,
it's up to us to spend all the cash
to be had from life insurance policies.

If we're not making enough money,
we can blame the glass ceiling.

Staying up till 4:00 A.M. Christmas morning
to wrap the kids' presents with your
husband and then saying, "We'll never
do this again." (Yeah right!)

I am a woman in process.

I'm just trying like everybody else.

I try to take every conflict,

every experience, and learn from it.

Life is never dull.

—*Oprah Winfrey, talk show host and actress*

No fashion faux pas we make
could ever rival the Speedo.

Getting to tell your parents you just
got your first promotion (Hey, we gotta
let them know all that college money
was good for something.)

Once a month, we have

full permission

to stop being so patient

with all the idiots around us

and let them witness the full force

of our wrath and vengeance.

Displaying an extraordinary ability
to color-coordinate clothes

As a little girl, you didn't rack yourself
on your bicycle all the time.

THE
JOY
OF BEING A WOMAN

Using pregnancy as an excuse

to eat *any* food we can scrounge up

during the day or force our husbands

to cook (This is something I completely

believe I would overabuse.)

If we're dumb, some people find it cute.

❧

We can *act* dumb as a means to
easily manipulate men.

❧

Heart-to-heart talks your children
initiate with you about their feelings
and what they're experiencing

THE
JOY
OF BEING A WOMAN

Noticing how beautiful

and sensual your nipples appear

in the mirror one morning

as you get dressed

Neither birth nor sex

forms a limit to genius.

—*Charlotte Brontë, English writer*

Assessing people just by
looking at their shoes

❦

Starting your morning off by catching
some of the *Today* show before you
launch into rush-hour traffic (I have to
also say I highly admire Katie Couric
because I believe she's one tough cookie—
more power to you, hot momma!)

We'll never regret piercing our ears.

✗

Learning to forgive those who have hurt
or wronged you over the years
so you can finally move on

✗

Wallowing in comfort food when
we're having a bad day and throwing on
a James Taylor CD

Openly chatting with girlfriends

about how much you adore

a radio station that specializes

in slow rock and love songs

You can wear a scarf and not look goofy
like Fred from *Scooby-Doo*.

⚘

If we marry someone
twenty years younger, we're aware
we look like total friggin' idiots.

Keeping up with your best girlfriends
by making time to sit down
and write them real letters

❧

Bitching about your catty sister-in-law.
Sometimes, you just gotta wonder what
is going through that broad's mind.

Women are never what they seem to be. There is the woman you see and there is the woman who is hidden. Buy the gift for the woman who is hidden.

—*Erma Bombeck, writer and humorist*

Being the subject of so many

beautiful portraits of the naked

human body over the centuries.

Two of my personal favorites are

Olympia (Manet) and *La Grande Odalisque*

(Ingres), which you can both see

the next time you are in Paris.

Sitting right beside a girlfriend
in a movie theater instead of placing
a seat between the two of you

❧

That quiet time in the morning when
you begin putzing around the house
before anyone else is awake

Accentuating your breasts
by wearing your purse diagonally
across your chest

❧

Rick Springfield's rear end
(This is one beautiful '80s icon.)

We can be caught crying at work
and doesn't mean the end of our
professional career.

Slapping teammates on the rear after
great sports plays is not expected.

Fashioning a turban with a towel
around your wet hair and seeing the
grin this ritual always causes
on your significant other's face

Having wings,
and I don't mean the kind that fly

✻

Getting to experience the special bond
breast feeding can foster between
you and your baby

Women have a way

of treating people more softly.

We treat souls with kid gloves.

—*Shirley Caesar, gospel singer and*

Grammy winner

Selecting bridal shower gifts

for girlfriends at Frederick's of Hollywood

(I always go straight for the sleaziest

thing on the rack because there's

nothing like making a good friend blush!)

A woman can get sex
whenever she wants it, period.

⚜

Curling up with your honey
for a nice weekend nap on the couch

Partaking in some ultra-juicy gossip

✕

Having a slumber party
with your girlfriends

✕

Woman cross-dress and start a trend.
Men cross-dress and scare off
their girlfriends.

The sophistication and style

we exude in gowns and cocktail dresses

at formal events (My husband is always

shocked at how well I clean up when

I actually get out of my blue jeans and

T-shirts occasionally.)

Wearing a lacy dress and looking
all innocent

Drying and keeping all the
flower arrangements you get from your
special someone

Doors are opened for you—
but if you want, you can open them
on your own.

Women have to

summon up courage

to fulfill dormant dreams.

—*Alice Walker, writer and essayist*

Instant sex appeal is but one step away. Just expose your nipples to something very cold.

❧

No one cares how long or short your hair is (unless you're part of some funky cult in Montana).

It's a pleasure for us to exhibit
good fashion and decorative sense.

❧

Filling out trashy magazine
questionnaires and making sure to rip out
the pages afterward so no one sees
your answers

Driving men nuts when you eat a corn dog

❧

You can dance with your girlfriends
at a bar or party. (And dancing with the
girls just plain isn't dancing with the girls
unless you request "YMCA" and
"Brick House.")

❧

Giving your male friends and relatives
great advice on the hussies they date

Telling a dazed expectant father that
it's time to go to the hospital

❧

The ever beautiful and delectable hint
of cleavage (And Tyra Banks, if you're
out there, I want you to know we
all think you got more than your
fair share!)

❧

You can wear a sweater-vest.
Men, they just plain can't.

THE
JOY
OF BEING A WOMAN

Because of their age-long training

in human relations—for that is

what feminine intuition really is—

women have a special contribution

to make to any group enterprise,

and I feel it is up to them to

contribute the kinds of awareness

that relatively few men . . . have

incorporated through their education.

—*Margaret Mead, anthropologist*

That silly feeling you get
when a date wins you a scrappy
stuffed animal at a carnival or fair

✼

Knowing you control the success
and fame of Michael Bolton and
David Hasselhoff

THE

JOY

OF BEING A WOMAN

Finding some unique stationery you can use when writing notes to your girlfriends (I'm convinced my friend Leslie would sell her soul for a lifetime supply of hip stationery products—it's just her top fetish.)

Feeling sassy while wearing thigh-highs
and garter belts

✣

All road trips must bow to our
incessant need for pee stops. (I'm drunk
with power on this one.)

✣

Ladies' Night perks at your favorite bar.
Granted they're ultimately to attract male
patrons, but hey, be glad it's not the
other way around.

Complaining about other women's unkempt eyebrows (My pal Jennifer totally confesses to this and declares she simply can't help noticing if a woman has Chia Pet—esque brows. On a side note, I've noticed that when I chat with her now, I keep my hands plastered across my forehead.)

Seeing your child upset after she's made
a mistake is a little painful, but it's
wonderful to ultimately know
she is learning how to make her way
in the world, one step at a time.

❧

You can be a belly dancer.

Getting ogled poolside

while in your bikini. I don't care

how much of a feminist you are,

you truly like getting checked out

while catching rays.

There are really

not many jobs that actually

require a penis or vagina, and

all other occupations

should be open to everyone.

—*Gloria Steinem, American feminist,*
editor, and writer

THE

JOY

OF BEING A WOMAN

Seeing the sign "SALE!"

❧

The shock given to husbands or
boyfriends the first time they see
you walking around the house in a
mud mask

❧

Having your young child exclaim
you are the most beautiful woman
in the world

Losing those five pounds
that never wanted to come off

❧

Seeing no line in the women's bathroom.
Nothing brings a bigger smile
to my face while in a crowded
public building.

Feeling a powerful sense of solidarity
as you run or walk with thousands
of other women in the Race for the Cure

❧

Spending Sunday afternoon with four
close-knit generations of your family

❧

Relishing that most kids say "Mom" first

Knowing why it is important to
line cabinet shelving and drawers
with Con-Tact paper

Snuggling with your cat, dog, or
lover as you wake up in the morning

A woman is like a tea bag—

you can't tell how strong she is

until you put her in hot water.

—*Nancy Reagan, former First Lady*

Crying during a movie and

slightly embarrassing your date

(In our household, though, it's usually

me *laughing* too hard during a movie

and embarrassing my date.)

Dumping a jerky boyfriend who doesn't appreciate you and congratulating yourself for having a backbone

❧

Surviving menopause and being able to laugh about it afterward

Dancing in pajamas with your daughter
before bedtime

❧

Getting even with the date
who dishonestly told people
you slept with him by informing
other women he has a very insignificant
you-know-what

Joining a convent (Okay, so it's not
for all of us!)

☙

Not acting your age by donning
Mickey Mouse ears with your children
at Disney World

☙

Our above-average diplomacy skills
get us out of nearly all speeding tickets.
I can't count on two hands all the
citations my charm has saved me from.

Understanding the whole
pre/post–Labor Day rule
about white shoes

❦

Making Christmas special
for your loved ones by not just
buying them whatever random gifts
are left at the mall on Christmas Eve

I wanted to be the first woman

to burn her bra, but it would

have taken the fire department

four days to put it out.

—*Dolly Parton, singer and actress*

Teaching your daughter how to
braid her hair

✻

Being a true romantic at heart

✻

Passing on family recipes to our
daughters, sons, and in-laws.
This is important because it initiates
a changing of the guard in the kitchen
that ensures you won't have to be the
one still cooking ten years later.

Being a charming and award-winning party hostess. I gain entertaining kudos by getting gourmet beer (anything but Meister Brau) and baking up some cookie dough at some point in the evening. (And no, friends don't think of me as a Martha.)

Your slinky dance moves leave men
desperate with desire.

❧

Getting over your
thong underwear stage

❧

Smelling shampoos in beauty product aisles
for hours on end. I cannot resist
picking up a bottle that has any
of the following words: *aloe vera, chamomile,*
or *coconut.*

Keeping bottles of lotion on our desks
and using them religiously

Letting the housework go and letting
the phone ring so you can carve out
a little fun time for yourself one afternoon.
Maybe you'll read a new book, maybe
you'll write a letter—who cares, just don't
pick up a mop! I love to curl up on
the couch and watch any HGTV show
that's coming on. I'm way addicted to
this channel and think they should give
me some type of frequent-viewership card.

A gentleman opposed to their

enfranchisement once said to me,

"Women have never produced

anything of any value to the world."

I told him the chief product of the

women had been the men,

and left it to him to decide whether

the product had any value.

—*Anna Howard Shaw, minister*

THE

JOY

OF BEING A WOMAN

Sending a friend a funny card that
so reminds you of her

❧

Getting to inform your husband
you are pregnant (and having nitroglycerin
handy just in case)

❧

Getting to tell your parents and
best friends you are pregnant and
getting bruises from all the hugs

Becoming a sugar momma
to a very energetic young man

Teasing a girlfriend when she finally
marries because she always swore up
and down she never would (My best friend
exalted in doing this to me.)

Discovering your daughter

has found your new tube of lipstick

and is covered from ear to ear with

Maybelline Strawberry Creme

and thinking she looks real good

Saying "I do" at your wedding with everyone's eyes upon you and your sweetie

Learning to distinguish who your true girlfriends are and appreciating them in all their brilliance, loyalty, and vitality

THE
JOY
OF BEING A WOMAN

Sitting down one rainy afternoon

to finally dig out your old pictures

and organize a wonderful photo album

that highlights your life's special moments.

(I'm so glad I finally stopped procrastinating

and did this, because I love showing my

albums to everyone now.)

French ticklers (Finally, something good
from the French.)

The foofy pleasure of occasionally
wearing bows or ribbons

True emancipation begins

neither at the polls nor in courts.

It begins in woman's soul.

—Emma Goldman, writer

Food day at the office.
There's something about having a
huge trough of food available that makes
for a better day at work.

You can flirt without words.
(I myself believe in the value of a
very sneaky grin.)

Finding a satin shirt that has a
beautiful sheen to it

Seeing fantastic women authors
on the best-seller lists after aeons
of our reading and writing abilities
being discounted

We beautify the world. We clean,
we decorate, we do whatever we can
to keep our environment pleasant
and relaxing.

❧

Seeing our daughters deal with their
squalling children in public and
knowing they're finally paying penance

Knowing a bouquet of flowers

is better than sliced bread (I'll make

any excuse to be decadent and buy

myself some irises. It's wonderful

having some fresh flowers beside me

while I'm trying to write.)

Making something possible for
your daughter that no one made possible
for you

✄

Experiencing the gentle yet mighty bond
of love between mother and child

✄

Playing Tony Bennett CDs during
your bubble baths

Life is not easy for any of us.

But what of that? We must have

perseverance and above all

confidence in ourselves.

We must believe that we

are gifted for something,

and that this thing, at whatever cost,

must be attained.

—*Marie Curie, French physicist
and Nobel Prize winner*

Hearing a little child say,
"I love you, Mommy."

✄

Beating a man at pool, an arcade game,
or some other traditionally masculine
entertainment form (I relish hosing
my husband in pinball!)

Redecorating a room and seeing

how your special touch made such

a big difference. There's nothing better

than overhauling a room that is

just starting to get on your nerves.

Slipping on a matching bra and
pair of panties. For one brief moment,
you feel both very organized
and ultra-chic.

❧

Electing to abstain from having
"third-date sex" with someone because
you suspect it may well be why you
were asked on a third date

Watching a close game of women's tennis
between the year's hottest ladies

※

We can display stuffed animals at
our workstations.

※

Sweet Sixteen parties (or, if you're
a Latina, your *quinceañera*)

You can ask men out on dates these days.
Heck, you can even propose.

❧

Taking a quiet day to peacefully walk
around a great museum, meditating on
both beautiful artwork and yourself
(I love the Art Institute of Chicago
and the San Francisco Museum
of Modern Art.)

For each of us as women,

there is a dark place within

where hidden and growing

our true spirit arises.

—*Audre Lorde, poet and educator*

Seeing your little girl proudly don

her Brownie or Girl Scout outfit

for the first time (which temporarily

makes you forget how darn expensive

the little thing was)

Dropping everything and taking a moment to hug your pet or child. I'm forced to do this a lot since my three cats all insist on "helping" me when I write. Dante strolls up to my computer monitor and sits in front of it (literally as I'm trying to type this sentence!). Sebastian jumps into my lap repeatedly until I make him a special place in another chair right beside me. And Emma, my beautiful female kitty, strolls into the room yeowing her head off until she gets some attention. Can't live with them, could *never* live without them.

You never see a woman

with a comb-over.

Having a gay male friend who helps you

with critical fashion decisions

THE

JOY

OF BEING A WOMAN

Turning around the houseplant
you thought for certain was beyond recovery
(By an act of God, I somehow managed
to reanimate a beloved fern recently.)

Somehow managing to pull off
a really good hair day without having to
sell your soul to the devil

We can talk to people of the
opposite sex without automatically
picturing them naked.

✥

Laughing at yourself as you witness
how freaky the nesting instinct makes
you act during your pregnancy
(In her eighth month, my sister-in-law
made her husband get up at 4:00 A.M.
one morning to clean out the refrigerator.
Why? Because it "had" to be done.)

The relief of finding the *perfect*
piece of clothing for an important event
you are about to attend

Having waterproof mascara to wear
for the day you go vamping at the pool

We learn best to listen

to our own voices

if we are listening

at the same time to other women—

whose stories,

for all our differences,

turn out, if we listen well,

to be our stories also.

—*Barbara Deming, feminist and political activist*

THE

JOY

OF BEING A WOMAN

Spritzing on the perfume
that makes everyone think of you,
be it Chanel No. 5 or Oscar or
whatever you've decided to make
your signature

❧

Embarrassing an entire group of
guys just by giggling with another woman

❧

Making a significant other understand
that biweekly trips to the shoe store
are standard procedure

Living to see the time when Mr. Moms
stay at home to be caretakers of the
house and kids

Getting to convert your child's
bedroom into a personal hobby room
when she finally moves the heck out

That perfect shade of blush
(To me, it's Maybelline's Sweetheart Rose,
hands down.)

The typical women's rest room
is infinitely cleaner than any given
gentlemen's room on the planet.

Modern-day sexual harassment =
Big lawsuit = Big settlement = You living in
Cancun up to your ears in diamonds,
daiquiris, and dinero

You always have the last word in an argument. If a man throws in a nippy statement after one argument has technically wrapped up, that just starts up a whole other argument that you'll have the final say in a few minutes later. (Don't let any significant others read this passage, or else the cat is way out of the bag.)

Giving your full attention to an important discussion with an important someone

A wise woman puts a grain

of sugar into everything

she says to a man,

and takes a grain of salt

with everything he says to her.

—*Helen Rowland, writer*

The relaxation that comes from
brushing your hair before you go to bed
(or maybe having a special someone
brush it for you)

❧

You can act excited about dressing up
for Halloween at any age.

❧

Your identity as a person isn't
ultra-dependent on what your
business card proclaims you to be.

The great after-workout high you
start getting after finally disciplining
yourself into an everyday exercise routine
after years of procrastination

⚜

Reading a treasured book from your
childhood to your kids, nieces, or nephews.
Tried and true and upon my own
bookshelf is a very tattered copy of
Shel Silverstein's *Where the Sidewalk Ends.*
Harm it and fear my hell-driven fury.

Living in an age where our daughters
have a stunning array of high-profile
female role models such as CEOs,
politicians, and brilliant entrepreneurs

It's possible to live our entire lives
without ever taking a group shower.
(Hallelujah!)

Ushering in the afternoon hours
with a nice cup of chamomile tea

Listening to any of Barry White's music,
and Marvin Gaye's "Let's Get It On"
and "Sexual Healing"

Wearing your ever-faithful pearl earrings

When I can't sleep,

I don't count sheep,

I count lovers. And by the time

I reach thirty-eight or thirty-nine,

I'm asleep.

—*Miriam Hopkins, actress*

Laughing when you see your
girlfriend become a wise, just,
cookie-baking mother after so many years
of being a sassy hell-raiser

✳

Silky pajama sets from Victoria's Secret

✳

Basking in a massage from a studly
Swede while wrapped in steamy towels

If we forget to shave, no one has to know
a thing about it.

Telling your child how much you love
the undecipherable arts and crafts
creation she lovingly made for you
and really meaning it

THE

JOY

OF BEING A WOMAN

Keeping a versatile color of lip liner
in your pocketbook in case
anything important crops up

�֍

Outdancing any date who ever
challenged you under a disco globe
(I confess that only one man came close
to giving me a run for my money in
this department, and David L., wherever
you are now . . . may the force
still be with you.)

Watching your children become
responsible and considerate, and patting
yourself on the back while trying to
figure out how you made it all click

&

Getting the perfect card from a girlfriend
right when you really needed it

&

Hearing the compliment of compliments:
"I absolutely love your outfit!"

THE
JOY
OF BEING A WOMAN

Show me a woman

who doesn't feel guilty

and I'll show you a man.

—*Erica Jong, writer and poet*

Lacy bras—there's just something
nice about throwing one on

✘

The impressive level of multitasking
you can accomplish while driving.
You dodge accidents, dig stuff out
of your purse, eat, talk on the cell phone,
apply lipstick, and dish out serious
road rage all at seventy miles per hour.
(And if you're me, you try to read
at red lights. And yes, I'm aware that's
a totally unsafe habit to foster.)

THE

JOY

OF BEING A WOMAN

Sidewalk sales in the summertime

&

Finding some candy in the bottom
of your purse that will bribe your
children into decent behavior for at least
the next ten minutes

&

Cheering your children on at their
basketball, soccer, and tennis games

Body glitter

(insert porn theme music here)

❧

We may never win an arm-wrestling
contest against a male counterpart,
but emotionally we're far stronger than men.
Sure, a commercial occasionally reduces us
to tears, but that's okay because such
sensitivity reveals our greatest strength—
that our hearts are always open
to the world.

Picking out your husband's clothes for him
so he doesn't look like a freak
beside you in public

⚹

Celebrating wedding anniversaries with
your husband and reminiscing about
the funny and tender moments of your
journey together (and thinking about
how he's still so darn *cute*)

⚹

Watching figure-skating events to
see women perform amazing feats
of athletic artistry and beauty

I believe in large families;

every woman should have at least

three husbands.

—*Zsa Zsa Gabor, actress*

Nursing your soap opera addiction

✁

Listening to any given Madonna CD. It's refreshing to have a female icon who just doesn't give a flip about the status quo and does what feels right.

After months and months of

botched attempts, finally executing

Grandma's potato salad recipe perfectly

and dancing in the kitchen to celebrate

(Unless you're me, in which case you just

feel fortunate to bring water to a boil

on the stove and don't even attempt

sacred family concoctions)

THE
JOY
OF BEING A WOMAN

Dropping by the gym and getting the high of working up a really good sweat

✿

Being inspired by a breast cancer survivor

✿

We can appreciate the irony of our conservative, old-school fathers telling us we can do or become whatever we want. (Then, we can prove them right.)

Relying on our deep emotional strength.
It takes *a lot* to make us truly break down.

Keeping alive special women's crafts
such as quilting, sewing, crocheting,
and canning. These activities are truly
becoming lost arts, and I encourage
anyone who could learn them from
a female relative to do so.

Lovingly mothering someone
who is in a crisis and needs a shoulder
to cry on for a while

❧

Doing a karaoke performance
with your girlfriends using any song
from the *Grease* soundtrack

There are women who

sit at home or hide their lives

in unfulfilling jobs because

they've believed stories

that they're too dumb, too fat,

too old, or too stupid

to fulfill their dreams.

We mustn't be afraid to be ourselves

and tell our stories.

—*Kathy Bates, actress*

THE

JOY

OF BEING A WOMAN

Discovering a once expensive
designer dress on the clearance rack.
I ain't talking Versace-level here though,
because you couldn't afford one of
those mothers even if it were discounted.

Keeping an ample supply of batteries
for your vibrators

Planning a surprise for your child

Confessing to your father that
as a teenager you dated wild boyfriends
just to drive him to insomnia

❧

Cuddling up with your dog and telling her
about your long day and how you hate
all the men you've been dating

Your husband picking out
a thoughtful gift for you all by himself.
I will never forget the day my honey
handed me a gift certificate for a full day
at my favorite salon. It blew me away,
and man did he get treated like
King for a Week.

❧

Reaching the level of confidence
that empowers you to stop depending
so much on makeup and clothing to
make you feel pretty

Laughing about the fact that a phone call
between two women never lasts short
of ten minutes

❧

Hearing a doctor say,
"You're definitely pregnant," after having
a *really* difficult time conceiving

❧

Bending over in laughter
as your adult children break down
and confess terribly sneaky things
they did as children

Where there is a woman

there is magic.

—*Ntozake Shange, poet and playwright*